sadness

To Madeleine and Maylis, who have also moved.
Affectionately,
G. T.

To my children and my godchildren.
V.M.
To all the children I accompany in coaching
on managing their emotions.
S.d.N.

Under the direction of Romain Lizé, President, MAGNIFICAT
Editor, MAGNIFICAT: Isabelle Galmiche
Editor, Ignatius: Vivian Dudro
Translator: MAGNIFICAT . Ignatius
Proofreader: Kathleen Hollenbeck
Graphic Designers: Armelle Riva, Thérèse Jauze
Layout: Gauthier Delauné
Production: Thierry Dubus, Audrey Bord

how to HANDLE MY EMOTIONS

Sadness

THREE STORIES ABOUT FEELING BETTER

Gaëlle Tertrais • Violaine Moulière • Ségolène de Noüel
Caroline Modeste

MAGNIFICAT • Ignatius

Contents

Introduction

Emotions—you feel a lot of them every day. Some are pleasant, and some are less so. Either way, they are an important part of the way God made you. They tell you how the world around you is affecting you.

In this book, you will learn to recognize the emotion of sadness: when you have a heavy heart, when your eyes fill with tears, when you don't want to do anything that you normally enjoy, and when life seems drab and colorless.

You will also learn not to let yourself be trapped by sadness. With Elliot and Charlotte, you will discover tools that will help you to accept this emotion, and the loss that might have caused it, and then to move beyond it. In each story—with the help of small drawings in the margins—you will be able to follow the steps taken by Elliot and Charlotte to see that sadness is a normal part of life and that through the virtues of altruism, hope, and gratitude they can find joy again.

1

A Friend Moves Away

Today is the start of the new school year. At recess, all the students are happy to see their friends again—but not Charlotte. She is having one of the saddest days of her life! Nina, her best friend, has moved away. Her family went to live in China, where her father has a job.

Charlotte sits all alone, knees bent under her chin. She has a lump in her throat, and she is trying not to cry.

CHARLOTTE NOTICES THE REACTIONS OF HER BODY.

Elliot comes running over, very happy. "Hey, Charlo, want to play kickball?"

"No, thanks," says Charlotte in a small voice. "I don't want to."

Charlotte is stuck in sadness. She feels like a butterfly caught in a spider web with no way to escape.

In the classroom, the teacher's voice sounds far away. Charlotte is lost in thought. She is remembering last year, when she and Nina sat next to each other. What fun they had! At lunch-time and recess, they would tell each other stories and laugh out loud. Charlotte's eyes fill with tears again, and again she holds them back.

After school, Charlotte goes straight home.

"How was the first day of school?" Mom asks.

Charlotte doesn't want to answer. She runs to her room and throws herself on her bed. Finally, she lets her tears flow freely.

Mom enters the room and sits beside Charlotte. "Where did that sunny smile go?" she asks. "What has made you so sad?"

Charlotte is sobbing so hard that she cannot reply. Her chin is trembling; her body is shaking. She feels that letting out all her sorrow is doing her good.

CHARLOTTE
WELCOMES
HER SADNESS.

Charlotte sits up, and Mom hugs her for a long time. Feeling the spider web gradually loosening, she whispers, "I really miss Nina . . . I wish she were here."

"You know," says Mom, "even though Nina is thousands of miles away, she is still your friend. You can you call her on Saturday, if you like, early in the morning. It will be evening her time."

On Saturday morning, Charlotte wakes up early to call Nina. She is excited and a little bit nervous too. Suddenly on the tablet screen her friend's face appears!

"Hello, Nina!"

"Hello, Charlotte!"

What joy for the friends to see each other!

"How is your new life in China?" asks Charlotte.

"The streets are crowded with people riding bicycles and speaking Mandarin," Nina says. "And the language isn't easy to learn. Using chopsticks isn't easy either!" Nina tells Charlotte that once, while she was trying to eat noodle soup, she splashed broth everywhere!

The two friends laugh out loud, just as before. But soon it is time for Nina to get ready for bed, and the friends must say goodbye.

In front of the screen that has gone black, Charlotte starts feeling blue again. Mom walks into the living room and asks for news of Nina. Seeing her daughter's sad look, she suddenly has an idea.

"You know our neighbor around the corner, Mrs. Parker?" she asks. "She called to say that she has a basket of apples for us. Would you like to go over and get it?"

"I dunno...," mutters Charlotte.

"It might make you feel better," says Mom. "Missing someone dear to us makes us sad. But we can find joy again by taking an interest in the people around us."

Alone in the living room, Charlotte considers what Mom said.

So now, what should I do about my sadness?

Charlotte is tired of feeling lonely, but she also feels stuck in the awful web of sadness. Could she break free by opening up to the people around her?

"I will visit Mrs. Parker!" she thinks.

"After all, I would like to make a new friend."

Charlotte stands up and spreads out her arms as far as she can. She feels herself breaking through the web!

CHARLOTTE PRACTICES THE VIRTUE OF ALTRUISM.

In the afternoon, Charlotte walks over to Mrs. Parker's house.

Mrs. Parker lives alone in an old house with blue shutters. Charlotte rings the bell, and an elderly woman opens the door. A warm smile spreads across her face. Her eyes twinkle with kindness.

"Come in, Charlotte," she says.

Inside, the house smells of waxed wood. Mrs. Parker leads Charlotte to the kitchen and shows her a large basket of apples.

"Did they come from your garden?" asks Charlotte.

"Yes. Would like to see it?"

Charlotte nods and follows Mrs. Parker through the back door to the garden.

"Here is where the apples came from," says Mrs. Parker, pointing to a tree. "Over there are plum trees and pear trees. Beyond them, I grow raspberries."

"What an amazing garden!" says Charlotte.

"Yes, but it's too much work at my age," says Mrs. Parker. "All that fruit to pick! Would you like to help me?"

"Why not?" thinks Charlotte. "Mrs. Parker is so nice!" The girl promises to return the following week.

On the way home, Charlotte realizes that she has not been sad all afternoon. The visit with her neighbor really did make her feel better.

The following Saturday, Charlotte returns to Mrs. Parker's house. Hardly has she rung the bell when the door opens.

"Hello, Charlotte!" says Mrs. Parker. "I'm very happy to see you. Today we are going to pick plums and make jam!"

Charlotte shakes the plum trees and gathers the fruit. In the kitchen, Mrs. Parker cuts the plums into pieces and throws them into a large pot with lots of sugar. As the plums cook, a sweet aroma drifts through the house.

When the jam is bubbling, Mrs. Parker hands Charlotte the large wooden spoon.

"Your turn to stir, my dear," she says. "I have a pain in my wrist."

When the jam is thick, Charlotte ladles it into prepared jars. Whoops! She knocks one over, and a big purple puddle spreads out over the counter.

"Oh, no! I'm sorry..."

Mrs. Parker quickly dips a finger into the spilled jam. She tastes the jam and beams. "Delicious!"

With the tip of her finger, Charlotte also tastes the jam. Yum, yum! What a treat!

She and Mrs. Parker slurp up the whole mess together—licking their fingers, smacking their lips, and laughing out loud.

After all the jars are filled, it's time to say goodbye. Charlotte hugs Mrs. Parker and gives her a big kiss on her soft, wrinkled cheek. Her heart is full of sunshine again!

At school on Monday morning, Charlotte feels as though she has bounced back to her usually happy self.

During recess, Elliot approaches her with a kickball.

"Hi, Charlo. Want to play?"

"Oh, yes!" she says, jumping up.

"You are very happy today. What's up?"

"I have a new friend! A cute little granny!"

"You don't think about Nina anymore?"

"Yes, of course I do," Charlotte answers. "She is still my friend! The other day, we even talked on our tablets. And we will see each other this summer."

Charlotte still misses Nina, but she no longer feels sad. She opened her arms and made a new friend.

To break out of sadness, Charlotte used the virtue of altruism, which is turning toward others to be interested in them, to love them, and to let them love you.

2

One Last Gift

In the long corridor of the hospital, Mom squeezes Elliot's hand to give him courage. His godfather is very ill. He will soon die.

Arriving at the man's room, Elliot is afraid to enter, but the voice of his godfather calls him: "Come in, Elliot."

Elliot rushes toward him and grabs his arm.

"Godfather!"

Elliot remembers the time his godfather took him to ride go-karts. They had so much fun, both driving around and around the track like crazy. Afterward, they had big chocolate ice-cream cones.

Oh, and the movies they saw together!

Elliot can't think of anything to say. He loves his godfather very much. Seeing him like this, Elliot guesses that they may never meet again.

His godfather looks deeply into his eyes and says, "I was waiting for you. I have one last gift for you."

"Oh?" says Elliot. "What is it?"

The man places a tiny round object into Elliot's hand. "This grain of wheat can help you find out," he says.

Elliot nods, even though he doesn't understand.

A nurse enters the room and whispers to Elliot's mother that his godfather needs to rest.

"It's time to go," Mom says. "Say goodbye to your godfather, Elliot."

With a heavy heart, Elliot tries to smile at his godfather, but his eyes are misty. He tries to say goodbye, but the word sticks in his throat.

Even though his godfather is sad too, he smiles at Elliot. He rubs the top of his Elliot's hand, the one holding the grain of wheat, and nods at him.

As Elliot, leaves, he squeezes the grain tightly.

A few days later, the phone rings. Mom picks it up, and by the face she makes, Elliot understands that his godfather is dead.

ELLIOT NOTICES THE REACTIONS OF HIS BODY.

His legs wobble as if the ground were crumbling beneath his feet. His chest hurts as if his heart were being pierced by a sword. Jerky sobs make breathing difficult, and he feels as though he is suffocating.

With tears in their eyes, Mom and Dad wrap their arms around Elliot. Mom strokes his hair.

At his godfather's funeral, Elliot lets himself be lulled by the music and the prayers of the Mass.

But afterward, as people around him are talking, he feels completely crushed. He tries hard not to cry.

Ever since his godfather's death, Elliot has been crying a lot, and once he starts, he can't stop.

ELLIOT WELCOMES HIS EMOTION.

Mom says, "Tears are good. Let them flow. They are like a balm to a broken heart." But Elliot doesn't want to cry anymore, especially not in front of all of these people.

Even though Mom and Dad are sad too, they try to help Elliot feel better. But nothing they say or do helps.

The next morning, Elliot can hardly get out of bed. He has no appetite. Mom is worried that he might be sick and takes him to the doctor.

"This child is in good health," says the doctor, "but he is depressed. He needs to be pampered a little."

ELLIOT RECOGNIZES HIS NEED TO BE CONSOLED.

So, Mom and Dad invite a few of Elliot's friends over for some fun. Outside, it starts snowing. How exciting!

Charlotte exclaims, "Come on, let's make a snowman!"

The other children join her—but not Elliot. He doesn't want to feel better. He prefers to remain unhappy. Through his window, he watches his friends playing in the snow-covered garden, and thinks of his godfather.

Mom walks into Elliot's room. She lays a big box on his bed and says, "Your godfather prepared this box for you, and I have been waiting for the right moment to give it to you."

As soon as she leaves, Elliot picks up the large metal box. On it is written: "Little Treasure Hunt." Inside, are four small glass jars, four bags of soil, four grains of wheat, and a fork! What does it all mean?

There are also several envelopes. He opens the one labeled "Today" and reads the note inside.

Dear Elliot,

If you read these words, it means that I left you all too soon. But I am here, with you, in a new way. To explain it to you, I suggest you plant the four grains of wheat, each in its own jar. Do not forget to water them and leave them in a sunny place. In one week, open the next envelope. I'm hugging you with all my heart.

Your godfather, who loves you.

Elliot has tears welling up in his eyes. He doesn't know if he's ready to be happy again. But he likes the idea of gardening. He plants the grains of wheat in the jars and looks forward to opening the second envelope next week.

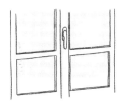

Suddenly, a snowball smashes against his window. It's from Charlotte.

"She'll regret this," Elliot thinks. "I'll get her!"

Elliot runs down the stairs and quickly puts on his coat, hat, and gloves. For the first time in a long while, Elliot has a smile on his face.

A week later, Elliot is all excited as he tears open the next envelope and discovers a notebook and another message from his godfather.

Dear Elliot,

I give you an observation job! Each week for the next three weeks, use the fork to dig one of the grains of wheat out of one of the jars. Just like a scientist, observe it carefully and write what you see in the notebook.

After three weeks, you will have one jar left. Wait a month before opening the last envelope and reading your instructions for the last grain of wheat.

Your godfather, who loves you.

Elliot picks up one of the jars and the fork. He carefully scrapes the soil to find the first grain of wheat. It feels like hunting for buried treasure!

Elliot looks carefully at the seed. It now has a tiny green shoot and three wispy white roots. He writes down everything and draws a picture.

He can hardly wait a whole week to dig up the second grain of wheat. Here is what he writes in the notebook:

The grain in the second jar is smaller than before, but the shoot is larger than the one I saw last week. It was sticking out of the soil before I dug it up. The roots are longer than the first ones I saw.

The next week, Elliot writes this:

The third grain of wheat has almost disappeared. The stem has green leaves, and the roots are long.

Only the last jar remains. Another whole month to wait! In the meantime, Elliot takes care of the little wheat plant by water-ing it. The grain of wheat has died, but the stem grows taller and taller. It forms a green cob with swollen kernels. Elliot counts them: there are more than twenty!

Outside, the snow melts. The days grow warmer. Little by little, blossoms appear on the branches of the cherry trees.

At last, the month of waiting is over!

Elliot nervously tears open the last envelope and reads the message inside.

Dear Elliot,

What remains of the grain of wheat? What happened when it died? What did you learn from it?

Well, you see, I'm kind of like that grain of wheat. Through death, I passed from this life on earth to new life with God in Heaven, a life full of love, like your grain-filled ear of wheat.

The treasure I give you is hope. God and I are always with you, and one day you will join us in Heaven, where there will be no more sorrow.

Your godfather, who loves you.

Tears roll down Elliot's cheeks. Strangely, they are tears of sadness mixed with joy.

So now, what should I do about my sadness?

ELLIOT CONSIDERS.

Elliot considers: Should he remain alone, stuck in his sadness? Or should he try to grow, to mature, and to bear fruit like the grain of wheat?

Elliot decides: he chooses to hope.

Hope in eternal life is the gift that his godfather gave him. To help him to hope, Elliot lifts his gaze toward the sky.

ELLIOT CHOOSES THE VIRTUE OF HOPE.

TO MOVE BEYOND SADNESS, ELLIOT USES A TOOL: HE LOOKS TOWARD HEAVEN.

Elliot runs to his room to look for the first grain of wheat that his godfather had placed in his hand. He hid it under his pillow, so as never to forget him. He reflects for a moment and then decides to bury it in the garden.

"There, it's done!" he thinks. "With the seed, I have buried my heart so that it can find new life."

The weeks go by. Every day, Elliot goes into the garden to watch the stalk of wheat grow. Gradually, his sadness goes away.

Two months go by. Elliot goes into the garden and calls his mother. She sits beside him and wraps her arm around him.

Elliot says, "Look at my grain of wheat, Mom; how well it has grown! You know, thanks to my godfather, I have discovered something: life and love are stronger than death."

Elliot chooses hope in eternal life.

With a peaceful heart, he looks up to the sky and winks at his godfather.

~~~~~~

To overcome his sadness, Elliot used the virtue of hope, which allows us to believe with confidence that in all situations God is with us and wants to give us life and happiness with him for ever.

~~~~~~

3

Charlotte Has the Blues

Charlotte groans as she looks out her bedroom window. "More fog!"

For a whole week, the weather has been gray.

Charlotte has only one desire: to go back to bed and stay there all day—reading comics.

Her mother wouldn't know, Charlotte thinks. She's out of town taking a class and won't be home for a couple of days.

Her father wouldn't know either. He usually leaves for work before Charlotte wakes up and returns in time for dinner.

He leaves her little notes everywhere:

There is butter in the fridge.

Don't forget to brush your teeth.

Work hard and have a great day, Sweetie!

Charlotte does not like being called Sweetie. And she is annoyed by these little notes everywhere. She doesn't want to work hard today. She wants to do nothing at all.

In the kitchen, her brother, Felix, is eating breakfast with his head hidden behind the cereal box. He doesn't bother to lift his head when Charlotte enters.

"He doesn't even say good morning," Charlotte thinks with a sigh.

She walks alone to school in the drizzle. Suddenly, the strap of her backpack snaps!

"I knew this was going to be a bad day!" Charlotte thinks.

As far as Charlotte is concerned, not a single good thing happens at school, and she walks home in a grumpy mood with Elliot.

"You're not any fun today, Charlo," says Elliot. "What's wrong?"

"I don't know," says Charlotte with a shrug.

"You are sad and don't know why?" asks Elliot.

Charlotte doesn't answer.

As they reach Elliot's house, he says good-bye and goes inside.

"He didn't even invite me over!" thinks Charlotte. "To make matters worse, it's still raining!"

Charlotte thinks everyone and everything are against her.

In her own empty house, Charlotte listens to the raindrops falling on the roof. She doesn't have any desire for an afternoon snack and heads for her room. The last few days her throat has felt tight, and she hasn't had much appetite. And she has been crying on and off for no reason.

CHARLOTTE NOTICES HOW HER BODY IS ACTING.

She feels as though she is carrying rocks on her back. She feels tired of everything.

"What's wrong with me?" she wonders.

"Maybe I'm sick. Yes, that's it, I must be sick with sadness."

The next day, Charlotte does not feel any better. For one thing, it's still raining. For another, it's Wednesday. "I'm sure to have a bad day on Wednesday," Charlotte thinks. "I'm only half-way through this long week!"

In the early afternoon, Charlotte has art class. Usually, she likes art. And the teacher, Mr. Thomas, often makes her laugh.

But today, Charlotte sits at her table without smiling or laughing at the teacher's jokes. Silently, she paints an empty, gray landscape.

Having forgotten to put on her apron, Charlotte smears black paint on herself.

"Oh, no," she moans. "I've stained my clothes! I can't do anything right."

Mr. Thomas walks up and says kindly, "It's not going well today, Charlotte; is it? What's wrong?"

"I'm sad," says Charlotte.

CHARLOTTE
WELCOMES
HER EMOTION..

36

Immediately, Charlotte bursts into tears. Teardrops fall on her paper, making grey halos on her picture. Charlotte feels a little embarrassed by crying in front of her teacher, but it doesn't seem to bother him.

"Would you like to tell me what's wrong?" he asks.

Charlotte tells him that her mom is out of town taking a class. Dad is always working. Her big brother never talks to her, and her little sister is annoying.

Mr. Thomas nods and says, "I'm sorry to hear that, Charlotte."

He sits on the stool beside her and adds, "You feel a little lonely, don't you?"

"Yes," Charlotte says with a sniffle. "I would like to see more of my family, but they don't have time for me anymore."

CHARLOTTE RECOGNIZES HER NEED FOR MORE ATTENTION.

"Hmmm, I understand," says Mr. Thomas. "Family life is not always easy."

Charlotte nods.

"Your parents are very busy," he says, "but I'm sure they love you very much."

Without another word, Mr. Thomas moves the water glass in front of Charlotte. He dips a brush into blue paint and then swishes it in the water.

"Tell me, Charlotte," he says. "What do you see?"

"A glass of blue water," says Charlotte.

"Is the glass empty or full?"

"Uh . . . it's half empty."

"You know what I see?" asks Mr. Thomas. "I see the glass half full!"

Charlotte is silent. "What is Mr. Thomas getting at?" she wonders.

"We can see the same glass as either half empty or half full," Mr. Thomas says. "We can see our lives that way too."

"What do you mean, Mr. Thomas?"

"When things are going well, we see our lives as half full, but when things are not going as well as we would like, we see our lives as half empty."

"So?"

"Seeing our lives as half empty makes us sad. Would you like to see your life as half full again and say goodbye to sadness?"

"Yes, I would," says Charlotte.

"Good!" says Mr. Thomas. "Then I have some homework for you."

"Homework?"

"Yes. When you go home today, think of all of the good things in your life. I'm sure there are plenty! Every time you think of something good, say thank you. Saying thank you is a great tool for dealing with sadness. It's called gratitude."

TO MOVE
BEYOND SADNESS
CHARLOTTE
USES A TOOL:
SAYING THANK YOU.

"What will gratitude do?" asks Charlotte.

"Gratitude changes the way you see things. Instead of focusing on what you don't have, you focus on what you do have. And you find joy again."

"You make it sound so easy," says Charlotte.

"At first you may have to force yourself to say thank you. But then it becomes a habit. Are you willing to give it a try?"

"I guess so," says Charlotte.

"Very good," says Mr. Thomas. "So, what are you going to say every time you think of something good in your life?"

"Thank you!" says Charlotte.

On the way home, Charlotte considers what Mr. Thomas said.

So, what do I do about my sadness?

Charlotte thinks, "Crying all the time is no fun." Her sadness is weighing her down, as if her backpack were full of rocks. She really would like to get rid of it.

At the front door, she makes a big decision: "Tonight, no complaining! Instead, from now on, I'm going to think of the good things in my life and say thank you!"

But, as soon as she enters the house, Charlotte trips on the front mat. Her notebooks, pencils, and paintbrushes spill out of her open backpack.

CHARLOTTE CHOOSES THE VIRTUE OF GRATITUDE.

"See! I really can't do anything right!" Charlotte moans. But suddenly she hears Felix in the kitchen.

"Yay! Dad made fries for dinner!"

"Fries are a good thing!" Charlotte thinks. She rushes into the kitchen, throws her arms around her father, and says, "Thank you, Dad!"

CHARLOTTE PRACTICES THE VIRTUE OF GRATITUDE.

"You're welcome!" says Dad as he hugs Charlotte back.

Already Charlotte feels a little better. "Yippee, saying thank you worked!" she thinks.

In her high chair, Charlotte's little sister, Anna, squeals happily. She smiles at Charlotte and holds out her hands toward her.

Charlotte kisses Anna's cute little hands and whispers, "Thank you!"

In the evening, in her room, Charlotte opens a small notebook and writes on the first page: "Notebook of Gratitude."

Then she writes down all the things she is thankful for today:

"Thank you for the fries."

"Thank you for Dad."

"Thank you for Felix and Anna."

"Thank you for my friend Elliot."

Looking out the window, she adds, "Thank you for the rain."

For the first time in a long time, she falls asleep without feeling sad.

The next day, she adds these items to her notebook:

"Thank you for the sunshine."

"Thank for Chloe playing with me at recess."

"Thank you for Mom coming home."

"Thank you for my family."

There are days when Charlotte's blues return, and she doesn't feel like writing in her notebook. All she can see are gloomy clouds everywhere. All she can feel are rocks in her backpack.

In those moments she remembers what Mr. Thomas said: it takes practice for gratitude to become a habit.

The following Wednesday, in art class, Charlotte shows Mr. Thomas her notebook.

"Bravo, Charlotte," he says. "Good job! You have found a lot of good things in your life, haven't you?"

Without saying a word, Charlotte fills her glass half full with water. She puts it down before Mr. Thomas and asks him, "Do you know what this is?"

Not waiting for his answer, she says, "It's a glass half full!"

Thanks to Mr. Thomas, Charlotte learned that by saying thank you for the good things in her life, she can turn her sadness into joy.

Charlotte used the virtue of gratitude, which is to be grateful for all the gifts and blessings in our life, including all the people who do us good.

SO, WHAT DID YOU LEARN FROM THE STORIES?

Sadness is often triggered when something bad or difficult happens to us. But sadness itself is not bad. It is the normal emotion that we feel when we lose something or someone very dear to us.

DO YOU KNOW? *There are many ways of saying that you are sad: having the blues or being stuck in the doldrums. Do you know any others?*

WHAT MAKES YOU SAD?
(Check the correct answer(s).)

☐ You lost someone or something dear to you.
☐ Someone you love has died.
☐ Everything seems to be going wrong.
☐ You are tired of being happy.

Write down an event that made you sad here:

....

....

....

....

WHAT DO YOU NEED WHEN YOU ARE SAD?
(Check the answers that apply to you.)

☐ I need to be comforted.
☐ I need to be listened to.
☐ I need to let time pass.
☐ I need to think of something else.
☐ Other:

....

....

....

VIRTUES FOR MOVING BEYOND SADNESS

To move beyond their sadness, Elliot and Charlotte choose a virtue in each story. Do you know what a virtue is? It is a habit of doing good.

At first, doing something good requires effort. But with practice, it becomes easier—like learning to ride a bike!

FOCUS ON PRUDENCE

"Be careful!" You often hear these words when there is some danger nearby. But being careful is not only about avoiding danger. Being careful is also about prudence, which is the virtue that helps us to choose our actions wisely. Prudence is one of **the four cardinal virtues**. The other three are temperance (self-control), fortitude (strength or courage), and justice (giving to each his due).

What does "cardinal" mean? Like the four cardinal points on the compass, **cardinal virtues point you in the right direction.**

As it is not always easy to practice the virtues, Elliot and Charlotte have found tools to help them. Find them in the stories and connect the tools to the corresponding virtues.

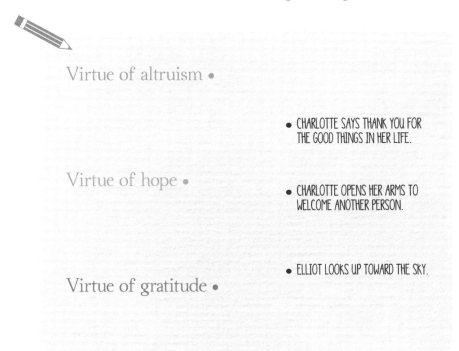

Virtue of altruism •

               • CHARLOTTE SAYS THANK YOU FOR THE GOOD THINGS IN HER LIFE.

Virtue of hope •

               • CHARLOTTE OPENS HER ARMS TO WELCOME ANOTHER PERSON.

               • ELLIOT LOOKS UP TOWARD THE SKY.

Virtue of gratitude •

now it is
your turn
to practice
the virtues!

THE PATHWAY THROUGH EMOTIONS

An emotion is a reaction to an event perceived by our five senses. It tells us we need something. Then it's up to us to work through it! To better understand what's happening, follow Elliot and Charlotte along the pathway of emotions!

I OWN MY EMOTION.

I ACT.

So now, how do I deal with my emotion? Let's break it down into steps.

1. EXPERIENCING A STIMULUS
Someone behaves in a way that hurts me. Something bad or difficult happens to me. I lose someone or something dear to me.

2. SENSING MY EMOTIONAL REACTION
I sense: my heart feels heavy; my eyes fill with tears; my throat tightens...
I feel: tired, trapped, worthless, lonely, and the like.

3. IDENTIFYING THE EMOTION
I ask myself: What am I feeling?
I realize: I feel sad.

4. OWNING THE EMOTION
I own the emotion for what it is: an emotion itself is neither good nor bad.

HOW WILL I HANDLE MY EMOTION?

8. MAKING A DECISION
I choose how to react. I choose:
to turn toward others, to hope with confidence,
to be thankful for what I have.

9. TAKING ACTION
I use the tools that will help me exercise virtue:
open my arms, say thank you, look up toward
heaven.

10. PRACTICING DAY AFTER DAY

10

9

HAPPINESS
Love, peace,
joy, respect, self-
esteem, and so on.

TEMPTATION

REGRET

8

6

5

I STOP TO THINK...

UNHAPPINESS
Closing in on myself,
losing hope, feeling
sorry for myself,
and so on.

How will I handle my emotion?

5. DISCERNING WHAT TO DO
I think about what would be good for me
and others.

6. RECOGNIZING WHAT I NEED
I need to be loved, to be comforted,
to be listened to, to let time pass...

7. SEEKING WAYS TO ANSWER MY NEED
VIRTUES: altruism, hope, and gratitude
VICES: selfishness, discouragement,
and ungratitude

VICE OR VIRTUE ?

From a young age, a child can identify his emotions, and by the age of reason he can learn to handle them. The purpose of these stories is to teach virtues that can help children with the emotion of sadness. When a child is sad, for an adult (parent, educator, teacher), adopting the right attitude is not always easy. Tell the child that this will pass? Recognize his sadness, minimize it, or ignore it?

HERE ARE SOME TIPS TO HELP YOU

Definition

Sadness is an involuntary, emotional withdrawal. It does not arise by chance but by some kind of loss or difficulty.

How is sadness expressed?

Sadness can be expressed through tears, but this is not always the case. In the three stories, we observe different expressions of sadness.

→ Charlotte withdraws into herself, cuts herself off from others, and does not play with her friends when she misses Nina.

→ Elliot cries and seeks solitude after the death of his godfather.

→ Charlotte loses her enthusiasm and her joy of life while her mother is out of town.

In general, when a child is sad, he drags himself around, he is folded in on himself, and his hands are closed. Sadness signals a particular need of the child.

It is important to take care of it.

THE EMOTIONOMETER

Sadness has different intensities. The child may be:

DEMORALIZED DISCOURAGED
UNHAPPY   DEPRESSED
DISAPPOINTED   DEPRESSIVE

How to accompany a child who is sad?

TO BEGIN, WELCOME THE EMOTION OF THE CHILD.

• Be fully available for the child

Put aside your cell phone and your concerns. Sit beside the child in a quiet place. It is easier to confide when we are side by side!

• Choose the right time

It is important to be able to talk to your child calmly, without being interrupted. It is up to you to choose the best moment: snack time, a trip alone with him in the car, in the evening at bedtime, and so on.

• Listen

Invite the child to say what he feels and to name his emotion. Some children will speak naturally. Others may need first to be cuddled or to be helped with questions:

What happened?

What are you feeling?

What is difficult?

The adult needs to help the child find the words but must be careful to let the child finish his sentences and to express his emotion for himself.

SWEETNESS AND KINDNESS!

Give the child your full attention. Lower the tone of your voice. Always let the child talk without judging what he feels and what he says! Avoid saying that his loss is no big deal.

You, too, as an adult, experience sadness. When a loved one is ill or dies, you feel sad. A setback or a disappointment can prompt you to feel sad too. Take the time to experience and to recognize your own emotion in such a situation. Give it a name and share it with your child so that he can understand why Mom is crying or Dad is less talkative than usual. It is important for children to see their parents modeling the behaviors they are trying to teach them.

• What is sadness for?

It gives us time to cope with difficult circumstances such as failures, disappointments, upsets, and bereavements.

HELP YOUR CHILD TO THINK.

• What does he need?

Help the child to identify his need: to be consoled, to be loved, to be encouraged to accept the situation.

• What should he do?

You are a guide for the child, but you cannot act for him. Advise him and help him decide what he can do to overcome his sadness:

"What are your thoughts?

"What if you ...?"

"Have you thought about...?"

Make sure he feels responsible for the choice he makes.

• What virtue can you practice?

Virtue can be practiced at any age! What virtues do you, the parent, practice in the face of sadness? The three stories in this book illustrate altruism, hope, and gratitude as responses to sadness. There are many other virtues: humility, generosity, delicacy, gentleness, prudence, patience, and so on. The child will learn them all the better if he sees you practicing them yourself. In this area, give free rein to your creativity! Take the virtue of altruism, for example: next time you have the blues, you can volunteer at a soup kitchen, relieve an overwhelmed mother by taking her young children to the park, start your own gratitude notebook, leave the biggest piece of cake for your spouse, donate lightly used items to a charity, write a card to a prisoner, lift up your sadness for someone who needs prayer, and so on. Many of these can be family activities. A loss to the whole family could be an opportunity to set up a piggy bank or to contribute to a fund to help others. The whole family could promise to practice a certain virtue and put a seed in a jar each time someone does.

A HELPING HAND FROM ABOVE

To advance on the virtuous path, God brings us his help and gives us his strength, especially in the sacraments. Christians can draw from the graces they received at their baptism, and especially the three theological virtues, which help with the exercise of all the other virtues:

Faith makes it possible to believe in God and in his love for us;

Charity helps us to return God's love and love others as we should;

Hope fills us with the confidence that, in all situations, God is with us, giving us what we need for eternal happiness with him.

And do not forget:

the virtuous path is the one that opens us to others and makes us happy!

⚠️ If the child continues to lock himself in his sadness, isolates himself, withdraws from life, or becomes depressed, do not hesitate to consult a professional who can help.

Printed in October 2022 by Dimograf, Poland.
Job number 23002
Printed in compliance with the Consumer Protection Safety Act, 2008.